Foreword

Welcome to the mosque. There are many beautiful mosques around the world with Islamic architecture and design that may vary from country to country. You may be wondering what "mosque" means. It comes from the Arabic word *masjid*, which means a place where you bow and prostrate. That is exactly how Muslims worship in a mosque. Muslims believe that they are standing up in the presence of God in straight lines and kneeling and bowing before Him in humility and gratitude. Peace and tranquility in the prayer hall help the worshipers focus on their prayers. While bowing and kneeling and reciting the verses from the Qur'an, they believe they are talking to God, who is listening to them closely.

On weekends, the mosques in America are bustling with life. You will see Sunday schools with children of different ages learning about their religion and participating in prayers and in many other educational activities. Every Friday, a little after noontime, you will see lots of people attending the weekly congregational prayers and listening to the sermon from their imam, the man who is responsible for leading the prayers.

Mosques are full of different social and charitable activities. People collect food for the homeless and donations for refugees or for victims of disasters. In America, mosques are also called Islamic Centers. The mosque in your area may have a full-time Islamic school where they teach the same subjects that you learn in a public school, but they also teach the Arabic language and the Qur'an and have classes for adults. There may be marriage parties and other religious and social celebrations going on when it is not time for the five regular daily prayers.

You will see lots of people of other faiths visiting the mosque to learn about Islam, or to attend interfaith activities between Muslims, Christians, Jews, and people of other faiths. Mosques encourage good relations by holding dialogues and discussions. This helps to promote mutual respect, peace, and harmony among different religions and communities.

Dr. Sayyid M. Syeed
Secretary General, The Islamic Society of North America

What You Will See Inside
A MOSQUE

Aisha Karen Khan
Photographs by Aaron Pepis

NOVALIS

Walking Together, Finding the Way
SKYLIGHT PATHS Publishing
Woodstock, Vermont

This book is dedicated to my family. Thank you from the bottom of my heart for the love and faith you have given to me throughout my life. Mom, you are forever close to my heart and a very important part of my life. Dad, I will always remember your caring heart and strong faith. Without my parents' strong faith, I would not be where I am today.

I especially thank my husband, Kamran, for all of his support—you are the main reason I sought and found such a beautiful religion. To my children, Burhan and Yusuf, whom I love so very much—may they always find strength and comfort in God's love. May my family and friends always find peace, strength, and hope in God, especially Nancy, Shirley, and Ken. Also, a special acknowledgment to Abdul Majid Khan and Rana Majid Khan.

SkyLight Paths Publishing extends appreciation to the Masjid al-Noor in Wappingers Falls, New York, and the Jerrahi Mosque in Spring Valley, New York, who generously allowed us to photograph their mosque interiors. SkyLight Paths also wishes to thank Imam Muhammad Asil Khan, Imam Muhammad Salahuddin, and the girls' youth group at Masjid al-Noor for their help.

What You Will See Inside a Mosque

Text © 2003 by Aisha Karen Khan
Illustrations © 2003 by The Pepis Studio

For information regarding permission to reprint material from this book, please mail or fax your request in writing to SkyLight Paths Publishing, Permissions Department, at the address / fax number listed below.

Library of Congress Cataloging-in-Publication Data
Khan, Aisha Karen, 1967–
What you will see inside a mosque / Aisha Karen Khan ; photographs by Aaron Pepis.
    p. cm. — (What you will see inside—)
Summary: Describes what happens inside a mosque and introduces the Muslim faith.
ISBN 1-893361-60-8
1. Islam—Rituals—Juvenile literature. 2. Islam—Rituals—Juvenile literature—Pictorial works. [1. Islam. 2. Mosques.] I. Pepis, Aaron, ill. II. Title. III. Series.
BP186.4.K44 2003
297.3'51—dc21

2002153436

A catalogue record for this book is available from the National Library of Canada.
ISBN 2-89507-398-8

10 9 8 7 6 5 4 3 2 1

Manufactured in Hong Kong
Book and Jacket Design: Dawn DeVries Sokol and Tim Holtz

SkyLight Paths, "Walking Together, Finding the Way" and colophon are trademarks of LongHill Partners, Inc., registered in the U.S. Patent and Trademark Office.

Walking Together, Finding the Way
Published by SkyLight Paths Publishing
A Division of LongHill Partners, Inc.
Sunset Farm Offices, Route 4, P.O. Box 237
Woodstock, VT 05091
Tel: (802) 457-4000   Fax: (802) 457-4004
www.skylightpaths.com

Published in Canada by Novalis, Saint Paul University, Ottawa, Canada
Business Office:
Novalis
49 Front Street East, 2nd Floor
Toronto, Ontario, Canada
M5E 1B3
Phone: 1-800-387-7164 or (416) 363-3303
Fax: 1-800-204-4140 or (416) 363-9409
www.novalis.ca

A Special Message to Young People

Mosques all around the world are different. Some are small, and some are big. Some are just square buildings, and some are large buildings with big minarets or domed roofs. Some mosques have beautiful, detailed Arabic script that decorates the walls, and some even have special imported tiles with Arabic and fancy patterns. However, mosques never have pictures or statues inside.

Masjid, an Arabic word, is often used even by English-speaking Muslims to refer to the building used as a mosque. To be a mosque, all a building needs is a *qibla,* an indentation in the wall that shows the direction of prayer, and a *musalla,* which is the main prayer hall. The most important part of a mosque is the people who come there. After all, a mosque is just a building. It is the people that make the religion.

Introduction

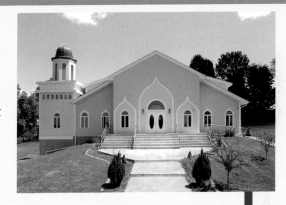

WELCOME! Please make yourself comfortable. Our mosque is a house of worship for God, but it is also a place to gather and talk about our spiritual beliefs and feelings. We gather to thank God in prayer for all that God provides us: our families, our food, and our health. We also take time out from our busy lives to talk with one another and to see how our friends are doing. Even though the mosque is a house of worship, in North America a mosque is also a place of community and a center of life where all people are welcome.

When Prophet Muhammad, peace be upon him, was alive, he loved having children in the mosque. He felt that it brought life to the building and to the community. He would sit for hours talking with them. Prophet Muhammad, peace be upon him, is an important person to us because he is a prophet, a messenger of God who helps people receive God's guidance. Whenever we mention the name of any prophet, we always say "peace be upon him" as a way of showing our respect. We do this in writing and in speaking any prophet's name.

Let's take a tour together of a mosque. We can explore the different rooms and talk about the different things we see. Come on, let's go inside and see.

The Call to Prayer

ADHAN: The call to prayer is spoken in Arabic and can be done by any Muslim boy or man. He holds his hands up to his ears as he performs the *adhan*.

"GOD IS GREAT. THERE IS NO GOD BUT GOD." These are the last words of the *adhan,* which calls all Muslims to prayer five times a day. The *adhan* is called several minutes before the prayer starts, to give people enough time to get to the mosque for their prayers. Then, there is a second call just before the prayers start. A man known as a *muazzin* used to call the *adhan* from the minaret, a tower that is part of the mosque. Today, if you visit a Muslim country, you will hear the *adhan* broadcast over loudspeakers. In North America, the *adhan* is called from inside the mosque.

We call our faith *Islam,* an Arabic word that means "peace." A person who practices Islam is called a *Muslim,* which means "one who submits to the Will of God." During our *salah* (the Arabic word for prayer), we prostrate ourselves, bending down to touch our foreheads to the floor. This is our way of showing respect and recognizing God as the one Almighty God.

MINARET: A tower that is part of the mosque, used to call the *adhan* for each of the five daily prayers.

PRAYER CLOCKS: The times of the prayers change along with the seasons. Muslims follow a lunar calendar in their religious lives. In this calendar, the months begin and end with the phases of the moon. These clocks show the times for each of the five daily prayers plus the *juma'a* prayer, the special noon prayer done at the mosque on Fridays.

Muslims perform five daily prayers. The first prayer is called *fajr,* which means "dawn" in Arabic. It is performed in the early morning just before sunrise. The second prayer, performed in the early afternoon, is called *zuhr,* the Arabic word for "noon." The third prayer, *'asr,* meaning "afternoon," is in the late afternoon. The fourth prayer is *maghrib,* meaning "sunset." It is performed just as the sun goes down. The fifth and final prayer, *'isha',* meaning "evening," is done at night before we go to bed.

A person can become a Muslim simply by saying the *shahada,* which is a statement of

faith and is said in Arabic. It means "There is no god but God, and Muhammad is the last Messenger of God." Saying the *shahada* and believing in it with your whole heart is the first of the Five Pillars of Islam, the basic requirements of the faith. The other four Pillars are praying five times a day, giving to the poor, fasting during Ramadan, and going on a pilgrimage to Mecca.

Peace Be upon You

WELCOME. *AS-SALAMU 'ALAYKUM.* This means "God's peace be upon you" in Arabic, and it is a very common greeting among Muslims. The first thing that we do when we enter a mosque is take off our shoes and place them on shoe racks near the front entrance. We want to keep the building clean so that we can do our prayers without worrying that the floor might be dirty.

Outside the main prayer hall is a foyer, a large area where we talk and gather before and after the prayers. Every local community centers its life on a mosque. Sometimes the mosque is called the Islamic Center or the Islamic Association.

After we greet any Muslims we see on our way into the mosque, we perform our *wudu,* a ritual washing that is required before doing any prayers. If we don't need to do *wudu,* we go directly into the prayer hall.

As Muslims we believe in Allah, the Arabic name for God—the same God whom Christians and Jewish people worship. Our Holy Book is called the Qur'an and is a direct revelation from God, revealed to Prophet Muhammad, peace be upon him, through the Archangel Gabriel in the seventh century. It is considered to be the main source of our faith, and it contains the laws and beliefs that we must follow in our everyday lives. The Qur'an is treated with the greatest respect. Although it has been translated into many languages, most Muslims read the text in Arabic, which is said to be the language of God. The original Arabic text always remains the same—it has not been changed since it was first written down. Mosques often have beautiful copies of the Qur'an that are enriched with Arabic script in bright colors and gold page decorations.

QUR'AN: The Qur'an is considered to be a complete record of the exact words revealed by God through the Archangel Gabriel to Prophet Muhammad, peace be upon him. It is the main source of every Muslim's faith. All mosques and Muslim homes contain a copy of this holy book.

ARABIC SCRIPT: All Muslims learn to read and understand Arabic so that they can perform and understand their prayers. Arabic script, containing words from the Qur'an, is used to decorate mosques and homes.

خَذْتُمُ الْعِجْلَ مِنْ بَعْدِ

عَنكُمْ مِنْ بَعْدِ ذَلِكَ لَعَلَّكُمْ

سَى الْكِتَبَ وَالْفُرْقَانَ لَعَلَّكُمْ

لِقَوْمِهِ يَقَوْمِ إِنَّكُمْ ظَلَمْتُمْ أَنفُ

فَتُوبُوا إِلَى بَارِيكُمْ فَأَقْتُلُوا أَنفُ

كُمْ فَتَابَ عَلَيْكُمْ إِنَّهُ هُوَ النُّو

نُؤْمِنَ لَكَ حَتَّ

Cleansing the Body and the Mind

BEFORE MUSLIMS CAN PERFORM DAILY PRAYERS, they have to make sure that they are clean, both physically and spiritually. The Qur'an teaches that we should be as clean as possible when we go before God in prayer.

There are a few reasons we will not be clean enough to do our prayers. For example, if we have gone to the bathroom or have just awakened in the morning, we will need to perform *wudu* before praying.

Mosques have special areas for men and women to perform *wudu* in privacy. They look like tiled bathrooms. Pairs of slippers are kept at the bathroom door for us to wear in the bathroom area. We want to make sure that our socks and feet don't become dirty. Because the main part of the bathroom space is used for *wudu* and should be kept clean at all times, the toilets are put in separate rooms.

LOW SINKS: We use these sinks to do our *wudu*. We sit on the small bench, which makes it easier to clean our feet without getting water all over the floor.

TILES: Some *wudu* areas have colorful tiles brought from the Middle East. In large mosques, the *wudu* areas are very large and can hold many people at one time.

When we perform *wudu*, we clean our bodies in a certain order, using water. Before we begin, we say, *"Bismillahir-Rahmanir-Rahim."* This is what we say before we begin any activity, such as eating, driving on a journey, or praying. It means "In the name of God, the Most Gracious, the Most Merciful."

After we say this, we wash our hands, rinse our mouth and nose, and wash our face three times each. Then we wash our arms up to the elbows three times, pass our wet hands over our hair and ears once, and wash our feet up to the ankles three times. We start with the right side and end with the left. When we are done, we say the *shahada*: "I bear witness that there is no god but God, and Muhammad is the last messenger of God." We are now ready to do our prayers.

Dressing Modestly

AS MUSLIMS WE FOLLOW THE RULES for daily life that God sent to us through the Qur'an. In the Qur'an, God tells us to cover our bodies. Dressing modestly is an important part of our religion. Muslim men and women alike are equally responsible for dressing modestly. This can be done using any type of clothing from any culture or country.

When we are inside a mosque, we are required to cover ourselves even more than in the outside world, out of respect for God. Men and women must cover the entire body with loose clothing. Men should also wear a topee, a small cap that covers the top of the head, and women must wear a scarf to cover the hair.

Although you may think that all Muslim women wear the long pajama-like outfit that is typical of Pakistan and India, Muslim women actually come from all different countries around the world. Many Muslims are born here in North America and wear outfits typical of our culture. You will see Muslim women wearing long skirts, pants with long tops, and long dresses. As long as their bodies and heads are covered, any style of clothing goes.

TOPEE: A small cap, usually round, that is worn inside the mosque by Muslim men and boys. It is usually worn during the daily prayers and *juma'a* prayers, but some men and boys wear one all the time.

MODEST DRESS: Muslim teenaged girls in North America choose modest but fashionable clothing and headscarves to show respect for God. Some girls and women cover themselves more than others. Some wear scarves all the time, and others wear scarves only at the mosque. A woman's culture often plays a large role in how she dresses.

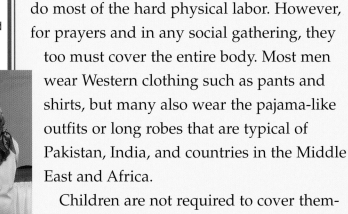

Men are required, in everyday dress, to at least cover themselves from belly button to knees. This is allowed because men typically do most of the hard physical labor. However, for prayers and in any social gathering, they too must cover the entire body. Most men wear Western clothing such as pants and shirts, but many also wear the pajama-like outfits or long robes that are typical of Pakistan, India, and countries in the Middle East and Africa.

Children are not required to cover themselves as strictly as adults, but boys and girls are encouraged to dress modestly. Boys and girls often wear topees and headscarves so that they learn the importance of showing respect to God while in the mosque.

Praying Together

MUSLIMS DO FIVE DAILY PRAYERS. Most of these prayers are done at home, at work, or wherever the person is when prayer time comes. But on Fridays we do the noon prayer at a nearby mosque. This congregational prayer is called the *juma'a*, and men are required to attend the mosque for this prayer. Women are encouraged to attend, but because of the needs of small children, they are not required to attend every week.

QIBLA: A small niche or indented area in the wall that shows the direction of the Ka'ba, which all Muslims face to pray. In North America, the *qibla* faces eastward.

In most Muslim countries, Friday is a day that people have off from work. Usually people gather after the prayers to talk and visit one another at their homes. In North America, Friday is a typical working day. We attend the prayers at the mosque and then go back to work. Some mosques offer a community lunch in the main foyer after prayers.

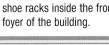

MINBAR: The raised set of steps from which the imam gives the sermon at the Friday *juma'a* prayer. Sometimes the imam stands at a podium next to the steps to give the sermon.

SHOE RACKS: Everyone's shoes are left outside the entrance to the mosque, to keep the floor clean for prayer. Some mosques have shoe racks inside the front foyer of the building.

Before the Friday *juma'a* prayer, the imam—the man who is responsible for leading the prayers—gives a short sermon. Like sermons in churches and synagogues, the talks usually cover a wide variety of topics, such as giving charity, how to improve ourselves, and how we should treat our family members and neighbors. The imam sits or stands on a carpeted set of steps to give the sermon.

Every mosque has a *qibla*: a niche or indented area in the wall that shows the direction of the Ka'ba, the small square building that Muslims consider the original House of God built by Abraham. In North America the *qibla* faces eastward. The Ka'ba is located in Mecca, Saudi Arabia, and is the holiest site in the Islamic world.

One difference between a mosque and other houses of worship is the absence of decoration. Mosques are often very plain. There are no special religious items or statues in a mosque. If there is any decoration at all, it is usually Arabic script or geometric designs that are typical of Islamic art. When we pray we do not want to be distracted by decorations or pictures. In fact, we cannot pray toward pictures of any kind.

Praying Separately

BECAUSE MUSLIMS BEND OVER AND TOUCH their foreheads to the floor during prayers, it is not considered proper for a woman to pray in front of a man. The man would see her in the bending position. Knowing this, it would be hard for the woman to freely do her prayers without worrying about her modesty. Because of this, most mosques have separate areas for women and girls. However, this separation is handled differently in individual mosques around the world.

Men and women usually enter the mosque through the same door. Once inside, women move to a separate room. In some mosques women have their own separate entrance as well as a separate room or upstairs balcony. Many are just one large prayer hall, where the men pray in the front and the women pray behind them, leaving a few feet of space as a separation. Sometimes there are partitions to separate the two areas.

Under Islamic law—the laws that are explained in the Qur'an—women are considered to be equal to men, both mentally and spiritually. All of us are responsible for our own actions, and all of us are expected to pray and do good deeds. Islam teaches that we should make a separation, both physically and mentally, between men and women during social gatherings and prayers. For example, Muslim men and women almost never shake hands when greeting each other, even if they are longtime friends or relatives. This separation is not meant to make women appear less equal. It is simply to create a social distance in order to aid the concentration of both men and women.

BALCONY: Mosques often have a separate balcony or room where women and girls can pray. This allows them to see and hear what is going on in the main prayer hall.

SEPARATE BUT EQUAL: Some mosques have separate entrances for women, or separate staircases to the women's area. Every mosque is different in how it accommodates women. During the time of Prophet Muhammad, peace be upon him, men and women prayed in the same prayer hall because mosques were very small.

Sharing What God Gives

AN IMPORTANT PART of being a Muslim is giving to others. We believe that everything we have in this world—houses, cars, money—comes from God. So, we should give to others what God has given us.

Every mosque has a place where Muslims can donate money to give to the poor or needy and also to help pay the expenses of the mosque. *Zakat*, which is Arabic for "charity," is the third Pillar of Islam. Throughout the Qur'an and the sayings of Prophet Muhammad, peace be upon him, we are told to give of our wealth and to help those in need in any way we can.

During the holy month of Ramadan, an important part of the Muslim calendar, we fast every day. If we are not able to fast for one of the days, we give the price of a meal for that day to a poor person. At the end of Ramadan, we also give the price of one meal for each member of our family before we celebrate the feast of *Eid al-fitr*. The money is given to poor families within the community so that they, too, can enjoy the holiday.

ZAKAT: The practice of giving money to the poor, an important requirement of Islam. Money is put in collection boxes in the mosque, or it can be given directly to the poor.

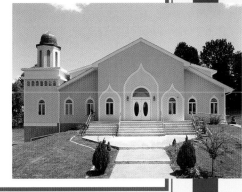

SADAQA: Charity that can be given to the poor, toward social activities, or any other cause. People also donate property or materials to the community—for example, to build a mosque or school. This is not required and can be given in any amount, large or small.

When we give money or help those in need, we do it without letting others know. Many Muslims quote this saying: "Practice charity so secretly that your left hand does not know what your right hand has given." In Islam, intentions are everything. No matter what good we do, it means nothing if our intentions are not right.

Collection plates or baskets are not passed around during the prayers. Instead, whoever wishes to give can put money into a collection box, which is usually kept in the main foyer of the mosque. This keeps the amount we give private—just between ourselves and God. Sometimes there are several boxes, each marked for a different charitable purpose. We can place money in these boxes any time we choose.

Fasting during Ramadan

THE MOSQUE BECOMES A LIVELY PLACE during Ramadan, an Islamic month during which Muslims fast. The Islamic months are based on the lunar calendar, meaning that they begin and end with each new moon. Ramadan is a beautiful month, full of prayers and family gatherings.

Fasting is the fourth Pillar of Islam. Every Muslim is expected to fast during Ramadan. Every day, we do not eat or drink anything from sunrise to sunset. Children, elderly people, people who are sick or need medicine to stay healthy throughout the day, and women who are pregnant or are caring for small infants are not required to fast.

Each day we wake up very early before the sun rises and eat breakfast. Some of us eat very big breakfasts with our families. Then we do our morning prayers. From that time on, we fast until the sun disappears from the sky.

We break our fast at sunset with a meal called *iftar*. Most people break the fast with fresh dates, sweet dishes, fresh fruit or fruit salad, and a drink of milk, orange juice, or flavored water, but we can break the fast with any type of food. Throughout the month, we invite friends and family to our houses to share this special time. *Iftar* is something we look forward to every day. Most mosques provide an *iftar* for people who are at the mosque to do their prayers. In Islamic countries such as Saudi Arabia, the very large mosques in the cities provide large *iftars* to feed the poor people in the community.

During Ramadan we are especially careful to say and do the right thing. Of course we should do good deeds all the time, but Ramadan is even more important because it is a time when God gives us a chance to be forgiven for our sins. It is a chance for us to try to become even closer to God. We read from the Qur'an every day, and we try to finish it before the end of the month. At the mosque every

LIBRARY: Most mosques have shelves of books on Islam, as well as copies of the Qur'an and also the *Hadith,* which are the traditions and sayings of Prophet Muhammad, peace be upon him.

PRAYER MAT: A special rug or mat that is kept clean to use for daily prayer. It is not necessary to use a prayer mat every time we pray. We can do our prayers on any clean floor.

night, there are special, long prayers after the *'isha'* prayer. These prayers sometimes take as long as two hours to complete.

We read a set of small books containing the thirty chapters, or *suras,* of the Qur'an. These books help us to complete the Qur'an, one chapter a day, or to read it all in one night by dividing it among several people. At least one person from the community stays in the mosque for the last ten days of Ramadan to dedicate those ten days to praying and reading the Qur'an.

Celebrating after Ramadan

AT THE END OF RAMADAN, Muslims celebrate one of the most important Islamic holidays, *Eid al-fitr.* It is a one-day celebration after the last day of fasting. In the evening on the twenty-ninth day of Ramadan, we go out to see if the moon has appeared. If the moon is not seen, we fast one more day. If it is seen, the next day is *Eid al-fitr.* During *Eid al-fitr,* we visit friends and family and have people over to our houses. It is a very happy and special holiday for children.

TRADITIONAL FOODS: *Eid al-fitr* tables are covered with favorite dishes from all around the world. Muslims come from many different cultures and eat many different kinds of food.

***EID* GIFTS:** Children receive new clothing, festively wrapped presents, and money gifts called *eidee* from their parents and relatives.

On *Eid al-fitr,* we wake up early in the morning and get ready to attend the *Eid* prayers, an event that is attended by most of the Muslims who live nearby. We shower, dress in new clothes, and eat a small breakfast before we go to the mosque. At the mosque, we greet friends and relatives and do a special prayer together. We also give charity to the poor. The rest of the day we go to see friends and relatives, and people come to visit us at our houses. There is always much good food to eat, and the children have a lot of fun playing with their friends. They receive presents and *eidee*—gifts of money from their parents, grandparents, and other relatives.

On *Eid al-fitr,* we see how much God gives us. After a month of fasting, we realize how important it is to have the food and drink that God provides us. To show God that we appreciate God's gifts and bounties, we prepare special food for the *Eid al-fitr* feast and set the table with our best dishes. Many of these favorites originated in traditional Muslim cultures, such as Pakistan, India, the Middle East, or Africa. We offer plenty of fresh fruits, which remind us of God's bounty, and sweet treats for the children.

Everyone gets new clothing to wear for *Eid.* Children love shopping to pick out an outfit they will wear on *Eid.* Parents sometimes buy their children outfits as an *Eid* present and surprise them on the day of *Eid.*

SHARE.

USE KIND
WORDS.

Thank
you!

SHOW
RESPECT.

I
one

he Week

Months of the Year

1 Muharram	7 Rajab
2 Safar	8 Shaban
3 Rabi'ul Awwal	9 Ramadhan
4 Rabi'ul Akhir	10 Shawwal
5 Jumadal Awwal	11 Dhul Qa'dah
6 Jumadal Akhir	12 Dhul Hijjah

Eid
Al-Adha

Eid
Al-Adha

Writing
Center

Y

Preserving Tradition

THE TRADITIONS OF THE ISLAMIC FAITH are passed along from adults to children. Muslims accept and honor all God's messengers and prophets who are known to us through the Torah, the Bible, and the Qur'an. Those who came before Prophet Muhammad, peace be upon him, were prophets such as Adam, Abraham, Moses, and Jesus, peace be upon them all.

Many mosques have schools where children are taught to respect these holy books and prophets. In the classrooms, children learn about the traditions and laws of Islam. They learn to read Arabic and say their prayers. They also learn about the holidays we celebrate in the Islamic year.

The holiday called *Eid al-'adha*, also known as the Major Festival, recognizes the faith in God that Prophet Abraham, peace be upon him, showed by his willingness to sacrifice his son when God commanded it. Since Prophet Abraham, peace be upon him, was so accepting of God's will, he was permitted to sacrifice a lamb instead of his son. The holiday, which occurs about two months and ten days after Ramadan, also marks the midpoint of the *hajj*, or pilgrimage to Mecca: the fifth and last Pillar of Islam.

Muslims attend prayers at the mosque in the morning and spend the day with family and friends. On *Eid al-'adha*, it is traditional to slaughter an animal and distribute its meat to friends, family members, and poor families in the community. Usually the animal to be sacrificed is a lamb, goat, or cow. In Muslim countries such as Turkey and Morocco, each family will slaughter an animal and give the meat to the poor. In North America, many Muslims instead send money to relatives living in poorer countries so that they can buy a lamb to feed themselves and the poor families in their neighborhoods.

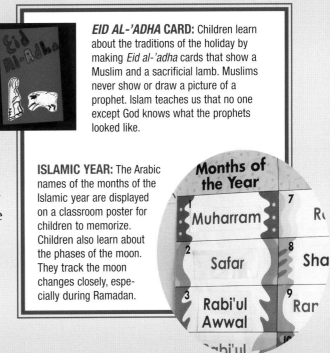

EID AL-'ADHA CARD: Children learn about the traditions of the holiday by making *Eid al-'adha* cards that show a Muslim and a sacrificial lamb. Muslims never show or draw a picture of a prophet. Islam teaches us that no one except God knows what the prophets looked like.

ISLAMIC YEAR: The Arabic names of the months of the Islamic year are displayed on a classroom poster for children to memorize. Children also learn about the phases of the moon. They track the moon changes closely, especially during Ramadan.

Months of the Year

1 Muharram	7 R
2 Safar	8 Sha
3 Rabi'ul Awwal	9 Rar
Rabi'ul	

Pilgrimage to Mecca

ONE OF THE LARGEST MOSQUES in the world, *masjid al-haram,* surrounds the Ka'ba in Mecca, Saudi Arabia. The Ka'ba is a small square building that we believe was built by Abraham when he was stranded in the desert. The Ka'ba is called the House of God.

The fifth Pillar of Islam is *hajj,* which means "pilgrimage." Every Muslim who can do so, physically and financially, must perform *hajj* once in his or her lifetime. Both men and women are required to do this as part of their faith.

To perform *hajj,* we travel to Mecca, Saudi Arabia, to visit the Ka'ba. Mecca is a large city that is also the birthplace of Islam and Prophet Muhammad, peace be upon him. *Hajj* is done at a certain time every year. It is a set of special rituals that are performed over a period of five days. *Eid al-'adha* occurs on the third day of *hajj.* When we finish *hajj,* it is said that we are cleansed of all sins.

Visiting the Ka'ba is the ultimate religious experience for Muslims. To us, it represents being the closest to God. Many Muslims break down into tears when they first look at the Ka'ba. It is a very spiritual and overwhelming feeling. Muslims save money for years in order to afford this once-in-a-lifetime trip.

During *hajj,* men must wear a white cotton cloth. This cloth cannot have any stitching or color, and it is held together with safety pins. This simple garment is a symbol that people are all equal, no matter what their income or where they come from. Women are not required to wear the white cloth because it would not cover their bodies. They can wear any white outfit or whatever dress is traditional to their country, but they must cover their hair, arms, and legs because they will be in a state of constant prayer and meditation.

We are not allowed to bring many things with us on *hajj.* It is a spiritual journey. Muslims bring along small books with prayers written in Arabic, which we need to know in order to do the *hajj.* At the end of the pilgrimage, most men shave off all the hair on their head. This is a symbol of erasing all their past sins and starting fresh.

WATER BOTTLES: Small bottles are brought to take water from the well of Zamzam in Mecca, Saudi Arabia, and carry it home. Zamzam is said to be the spring of water that gushed from the desert sand when Ishma'il (son of the Prophet Abraham, peace be upon him) stomped his foot on the ground out of thirst, when he and his mother, Hagar, were stranded in the desert.

SPECIAL BELT: Because the white cloth that they wear has no pockets, men sometimes wear special belts to carry their money, passports, and books containing prayers.

PINS: The white garments are held together by safety pins, since no sewing is allowed.

KA'BA: The small square building in Mecca, Saudi Arabia, that Muslims consider to be the original House of God built by Abraham. Each year it is covered with a new black cloth on which are stitched verses from the Qur'an.

Practice Makes Perfect

PROPHET MUHAMMAD, peace be upon him, is the ultimate example of how Muslims should live their lives. Much as Jesus is an example to Christians, Muslims try to follow the example of Prophet Muhammad, peace be upon him, by studying how he lived his life, performed his prayers, and dealt with friends, family members, and neighbors.

To do this, Muslims often refer to a collection of books called the *Hadith*. The *Hadith* is a collection of the sayings and behaviors of Prophet Muhammad, peace be upon him, telling us how he lived his life and how he practiced Islam. For example, it is from the *Hadith* that we know how to perform our prayers.

All Muslims are required to learn about their religion and to learn how to perform their prayers. By the time boys and girls turn seven years old, they are expected to be able to per-form their prayers and understand the basics of their religion.

Since the prayers are all recited in Arabic, every Muslim has to learn to read and recite

CONCENTRATION: Learning the Arabic alphabet takes a lot of concentration and study. Books in Arabic read from right to left on each page, similar to Hebrew. The correct pronunciation is a skill that takes years to master.

QUR'AN STUDY: Boys and girls are expected to be able to at least read parts of the Qur'an on their own by the time they are seven years old.

Arabic, and this sometimes begins as early as age three. Many mosques have religious teachers who help children memorize the prayers and learn the Arabic language. Most mosques have a space set apart for teaching and learning—or even simply reading the Qur'an before or after the time for prayers. There are wooden bookstands to keep the books open flat for reading, and there are simple wooden benches on which we can rest the books while we kneel or sit on the floor. Large pillows and cushions can also make the reading area more comfortable.

When children begin to read the Qur'an, the family usually has a small celebration called a *Bismillah,* and when a child completes reading the Qur'an, the family usually holds a celebration called an *Amin.*

Learning about Islam

ISLAM IS A RELIGION THAT EXPECTS LEARNING. As Muslims, we have a responsibility to learn as much as we can about our religion and our world. Just like churches, synagogues, and other religious buildings, mosques also have libraries, Sunday schools, full-time schools, and classes during the week to teach Muslim children and adults about their religion and the Islamic way of life.

Because learning is so important, you will find a lot of books and Qur'ans in mosques and Islamic centers. Sometimes the books are contained in a library or reading room with shelves and comfortable seating areas. The books are often beautifully bound in hard covers with gold decorative lettering. They are written in Arabic, English, and other languages that are spoken in the various Muslim countries.

The Qur'an has been translated into many languages so that people from all over the world can read and understand it. Most versions of the Qur'an contain the original Arabic script. Some have the Arabic words and another language such as English on the opposite side of the page. It is very important to read the Qur'an in the original language in which it was given to Prophet Muhammad, peace be upon him. That is why Muslims of every nation learn to read Arabic.

IMAM: A man who has studied the Qur'an and *Hadith* and has a strong understanding of the Islamic religion and its practices. Often he leads the prayers.

WALL HANGINGS: Passages from the Qur'an and other holy books beautifully written in Arabic script and displayed on the mosque's walls to keep the words of the Prophet, peace be upon him, in our minds at all times.

A Place to Pray

THE RELIGION OF ISLAM TEACHES us that we should always think about God, do good deeds, and speak kind words. God has told us to pray five times a day. This helps us to remember God's goodness. It makes us stop and think about what is right and wrong, and it gives us the strength to get through hard days.

Praying the five daily prayers is one of the Five Pillars of Islam. Although it is ideal for us to do our prayers at a mosque, Muslims can do their prayers anywhere. We often use small rugs called prayer mats to make sure that the floor is clean where we pray. Since prayers in a house or building can be done anywhere, we do not wear shoes inside our homes or mosques.

The prayer rug or mat is a small carpet that is placed on the floor when we do our prayers. In our homes, we usually fold up the prayer rug when we are not using it, to keep it clean. In the mosque, most prayer rugs are tacked down to the carpet. This helps Muslims form a straight line during large gatherings for prayers.

TILED *QIBLA:* This *qibla* is made of tiles brought from Turkey. Plain or fancy, the *qibla* directs our prayer toward the Ka'ba in Mecca.

PRAYER POSITIONS: Each stage of the daily prayer is performed in a different position, from standing to bowing to prostrating to sitting. Touching the forehead to the floor shows that we are humble before God.

If we are not able to bend down to the floor to perform our prayers, we can sit in a chair. We can even lie in bed if we are too sick to sit up. If we are traveling, we can do the prayers while riding in a car or on a bus. In a city you may see a line of Muslim taxi drivers on their prayer mats on the sidewalk in front of the taxi stand, all facing toward Mecca. A mosque is a wonderful place to pray, but what is most important is the prayer itself.

About SkyLight Paths

SkyLight Paths is creating a place where children and adults of different spiritual traditions come together for challenge and inspiration, a place where we can help each other understand the mystery that lies at the heart of our existence.

SkyLight Paths creates beautiful books for believers and seekers of any age, a community that increasingly transcends the traditional boundaries of religion and denomination—people wanting to learn from each other, walking together, finding the way.